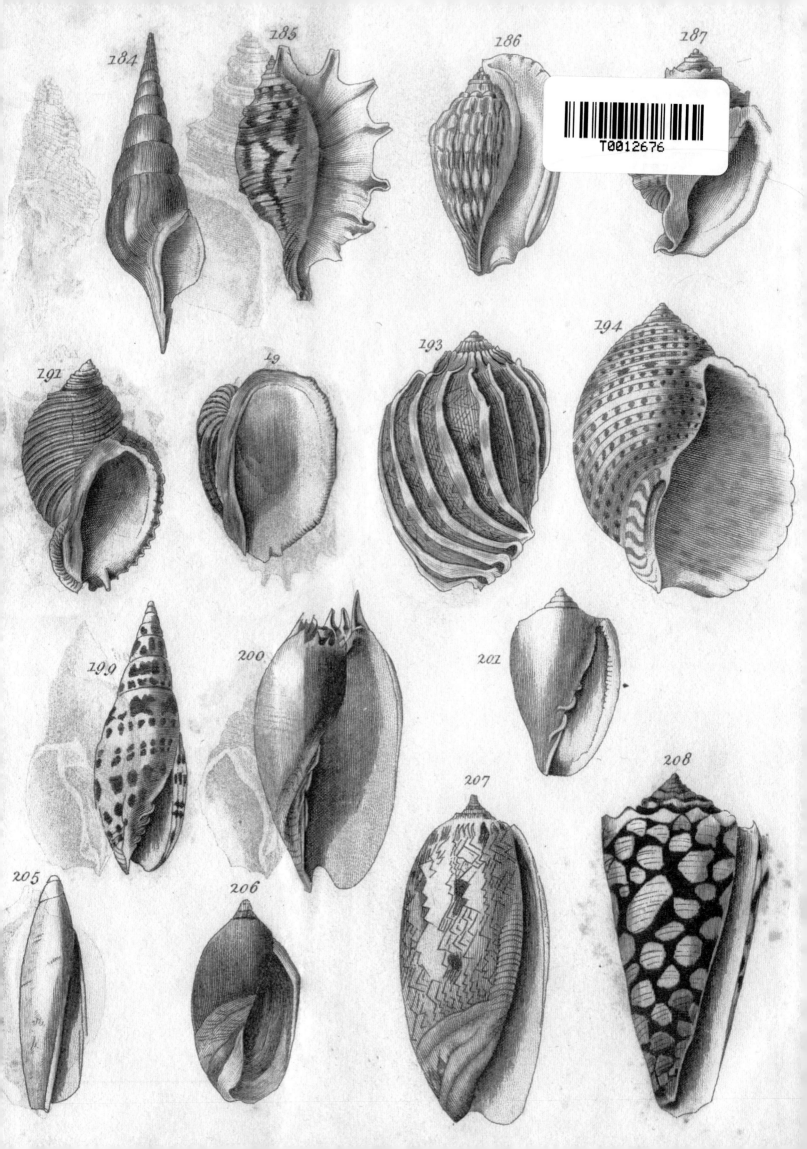

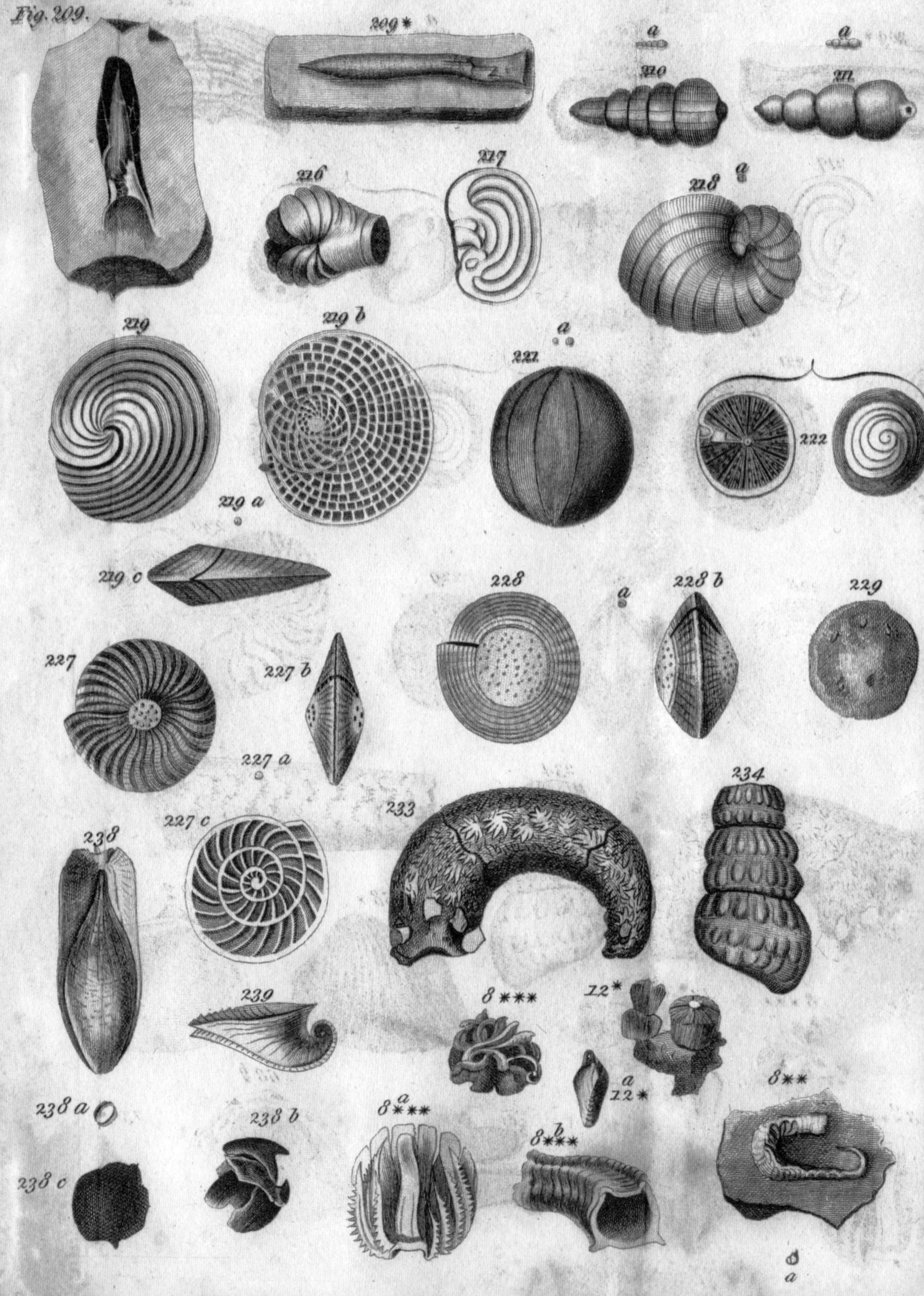

Fig. 209.

209*

a   a

210   211

226   227   228

219   219 b   227   222

219 a

219 c   228   228 b   229

227

227 b

227 a

238   227 c   233   234

239   8 ***   12*

a
12*

8 **

238 a

238 b   8 a ***

8 b ***

238 c   a

The Bluest of Blues

Anna Atkins and the First
Book of Photographs

By Fiona Robinson

Abrams Books for Young Readers
New York

1807—The English Meadow

The sky is the bluest of blues.

Little Anna's arms are full of flowers: buttercups,
forget-me-nots, corncockles, love-in-a-mist, feverfew, and
marigolds. The air is thick with butterflies and bees.
Father carries a jar of clambering insects. A heavy book
weighs down his coat.

Anna finds a poppy.

She wants to keep the poppy forever. Father passes her the book. She opens it and places the poppy on the pages. She closes the cover, pressing the flower flat. It will dry there, between the pages, preserved for her to examine later.

Father claps in delight.

The Laboratory

When they return home, Anna and Father examine the insects. He is a scientist and has a laboratory in their home in Tonbridge, England. Aside from experimenting with electricity and chemicals, he is fascinated by entomology—the scientific study of insects. He has thousands upon thousands of them!

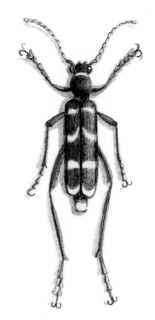

Clytus arietus

Crioceris asparagi

Anna gently curls and twists her hand as a tiny, spotted beetle skitters around and tickles her fingers.

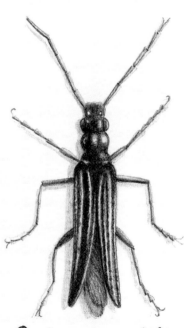

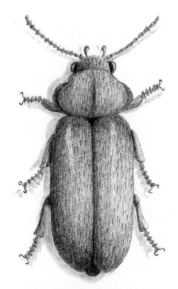

Xestobium
rufovillosum

Staphylinus olens

Oedemera nobilis

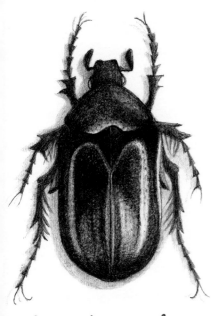

Cetonia aurata

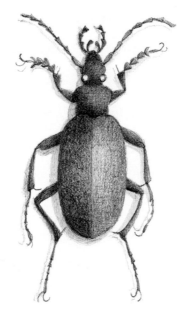

Carabus violaceus

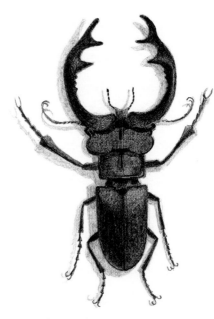

Lucanus cervus

Father explains that although this insect is small, it has dozens of different names around the world. In England, it is known as a *ladybird*. In America, it is a *ladybug*. The French call it a *coccinelle*. The Japanese, a *tentoumushi*!

But Father tells Anna that the many species of the ladybird family all have one special scientific or Latin name, Coccinellidae.

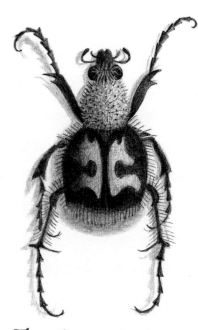

Trichius fasciatus

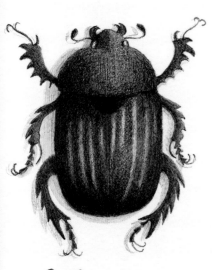

Geotropes stercorarius

This naming system was created more than seventy years before, in 1735, so that scientists from different countries could discuss their research with less confusion. Latin was the language chosen to label every plant and animal in the world.

Coccinella septempunctata

Father's name is John
Children, but his only child
is Anna. Anna's mother died
soon after her birth in 1799.

Father is determined to give his daughter the best education in
the world at a time when few girls receive any schooling at all. He
will teach her the sciences: chemistry, physics, zoology, botany, and
biology. And, of course, the naming language of science, Latin.

She is his beloved child but also his partner in research. She, too, is fascinated by collecting specimens to name and study.

On this day, she lays her flowers on a table and sifts through them, observing closely their different leaves and petals.

1811—Beside the Sea

The sea is the bluest of blues.

Anna finds a long strip of squeaky, bubbly, brown seaweed.

"*Fucus vesiculosus!*" states Father.

"*Fu-cus ve-sic-u-lo-sus!*" says Anna, repeating the Latin carefully.

She takes the seaweed by its roots and swings it high above her head. Momentarily, she sees it silhouetted against the bluest of blues.

She places the seaweed with her other treasures from the day.

Seaweeds: bladderwrack, kelp, Irish moss, dead man's bootlaces, landlady's wig.

Shells: razor, periwinkle, limpet, cockle, barnacle, cowrie, scallop.

There's driftwood, too. And dogfish eggs that are also called mermaid's purses. And cuttlefish bones that the birds feast on.

Anna takes out her notebook. She draws and records the seaweeds: bubbles and bobbles, tendrils and roots, frizzes and wrinkles. Father helps her label them with their scientific names.

Anna is a treasure hunter. Anna is an artist. Anna is a scientist!

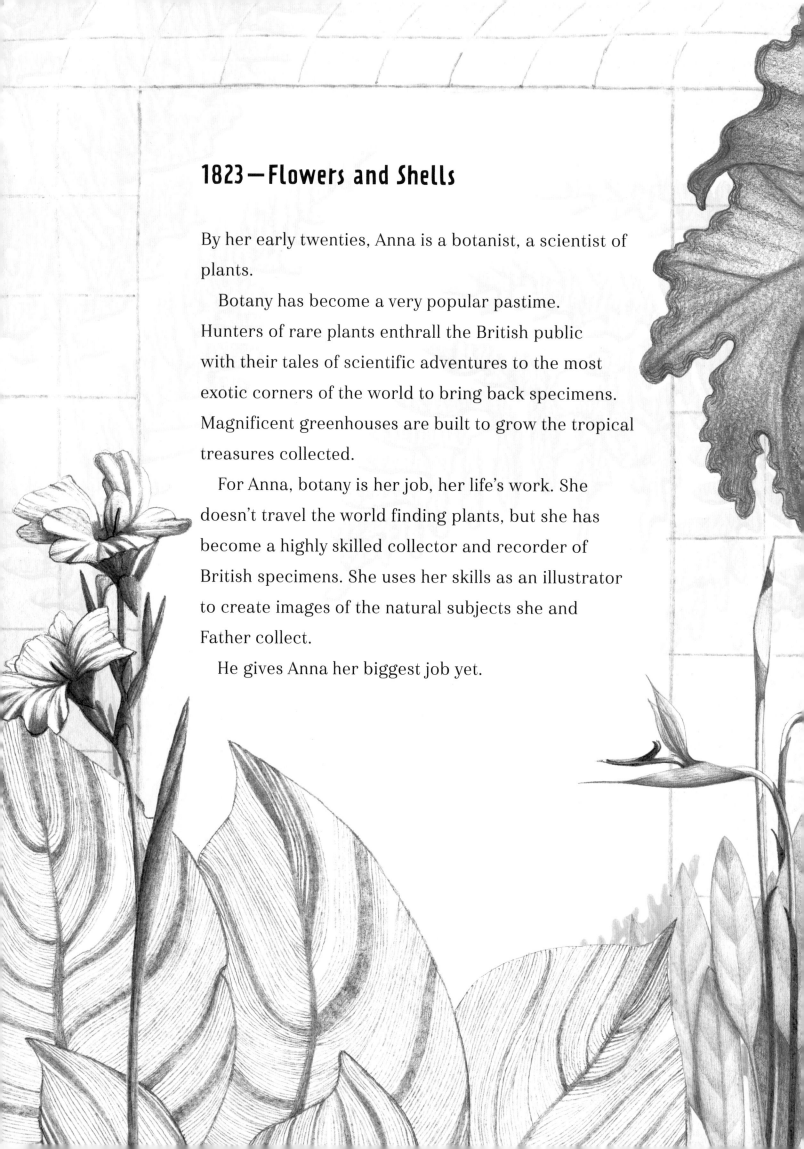

1823—Flowers and Shells

By her early twenties, Anna is a botanist, a scientist of plants.

Botany has become a very popular pastime. Hunters of rare plants enthrall the British public with their tales of scientific adventures to the most exotic corners of the world to bring back specimens. Magnificent greenhouses are built to grow the tropical treasures collected.

For Anna, botany is her job, her life's work. She doesn't travel the world finding plants, but she has become a highly skilled collector and recorder of British specimens. She uses her skills as an illustrator to create images of the natural subjects she and Father collect.

He gives Anna her biggest job yet.

He has just translated articles from French scientific journals into English.

Titled *Lamarck's Genera of Shells*, the series is a guide describing and scientifically labelling shells. But something is missing that would greatly improve identification—illustrations! He asks Anna to help.

On this day, Anna holds a long, curved, ridged shell.

It's an elephant-tusk shell from the Philippines. It will take her several hours to capture it in pencil. Anna's drawing must be as perfectly lifelike as humanly possible. An engraver will copy her image onto a printing plate for publication.

She has more than 250 illustrations to complete.

1825 — Love and London

Anna marries John Pelly Atkins and becomes Anna Atkins.
He is the son of the former Lord Mayor of London and
a wealthy merchant. They live in London near Father,
who now works in the Natural History Department at the
British Museum.

Father is a busy man, although he tries to see Anna
most days. He is a fellow of the Royal Society of London
for Improving Natural Knowledge.

The Society holds lectures and publishes papers
on everything new in science: thermometers, comets,
meteors, exploding rockets, magnetism, geometry,
disease, longitude and latitude, the circulation of blood in
insects, tides, EVERYTHING.

The Society is an important meeting place for
scientists to discuss their work. But women aren't allowed.
Father recounts important lectures to Anna. He passes on
papers to her. But when will she get to share her knowledge
of the natural world with the scientific community?

Anna dedicates
herself to creating an
herbarium, a collection of dried plants.
In a room filled with large storage chests,
she uses a flower press to flatten and preserve
seaweed, lichen, ferns, and flowering plants of
the British Isles. It is a massive task. Each
individual specimen, once
flat and dried, is mounted on
paper and placed in a drawer
for protection.

She is proud of
her herbarium, but it is
not accessible to a wide
audience. Illustrating and
publishing it would take far too long—her seaweed
collection alone amounts to over 1,500 examples!

Anna thinks, if only there was a
quick, accurate way to copy
her collection . . .

In 1839, she is granted membership to the Royal Botanic
Society in London, one of the few institutions at the time to admit women.
It is a great achievement.

1841—The Gift

When Father retires, he, Anna, and her husband, John, move to the Kent countryside together. Father takes up astronomy, studying the night sky. But he and Anna share a passion for a new invention— photography! For Anna especially, it is a wonderful combination: part science—involving the use of light-sensitive chemicals—and part art—involving the careful composition of a subject.

One morning at breakfast, Father places a wooden box on Anna's lap. She turns it around carefully. There's a slot at the top and a hole in one side where a circle of glass sits.

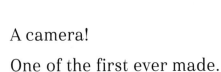

A camera!
One of the first ever made.

Anna and Father spend many hours together experimenting. It is both exciting and hard work.

The word *photography* literally means "drawing with light." Most of their endeavors require the strongest source of light known to people—the sun.

None of
Anna's early
photographs
survive today.
The prints faded
over time, like
memories.

But she is now
acknowledged to be
one of the first women
in the world to take a
photograph!

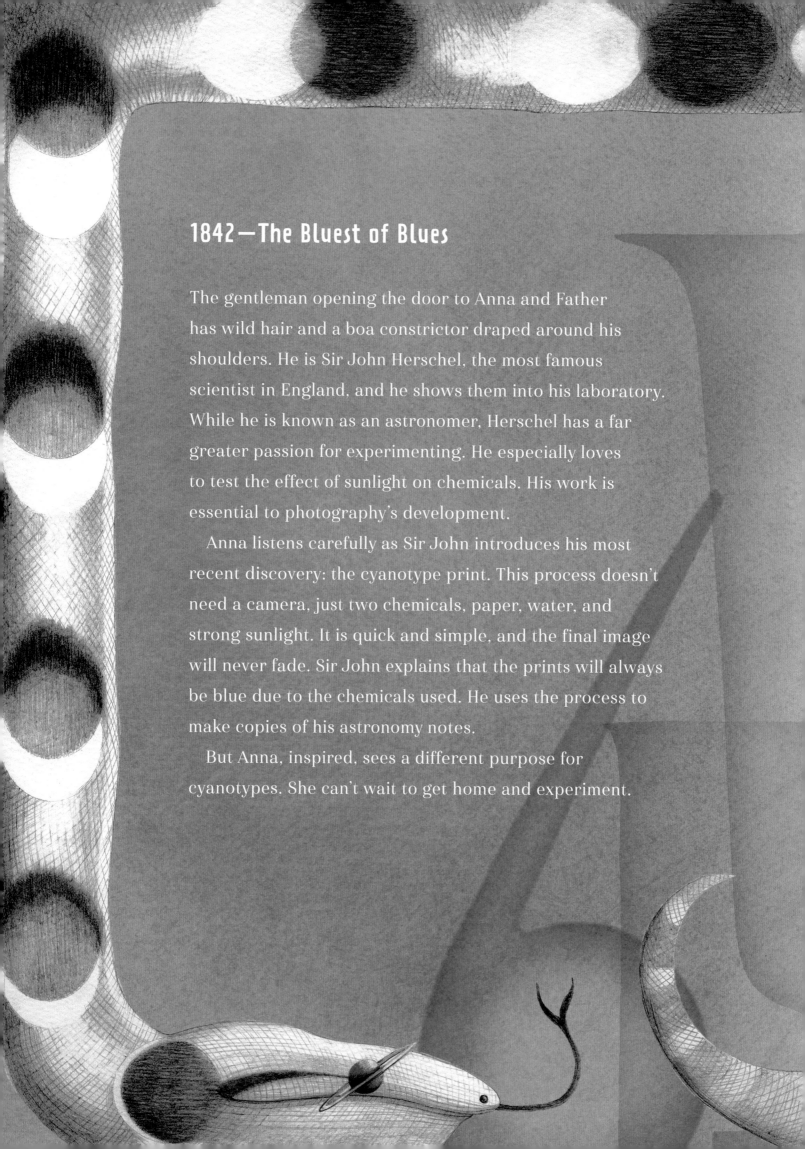

1842—The Bluest of Blues

The gentleman opening the door to Anna and Father has wild hair and a boa constrictor draped around his shoulders. He is Sir John Herschel, the most famous scientist in England, and he shows them into his laboratory. While he is known as an astronomer, Herschel has a far greater passion for experimenting. He especially loves to test the effect of sunlight on chemicals. His work is essential to photography's development.

Anna listens carefully as Sir John introduces his most recent discovery: the cyanotype print. This process doesn't need a camera, just two chemicals, paper, water, and strong sunlight. It is quick and simple, and the final image will never fade. Sir John explains that the prints will always be blue due to the chemicals used. He uses the process to make copies of his astronomy notes.

But Anna, inspired, sees a different purpose for cyanotypes. She can't wait to get home and experiment.

In a dark room, Anna coats paper with a mixture of ammonium iron citrate and potassium ferricyanide.

She takes the paper outside and lays it down to bathe in the bright sun's rays.

She arranges a piece of seaweed from her herbarium on the paper and places a sheet of glass on top.
She waits a few minutes.

She removes the seaweed
and soaks the paper in water.

As if by magic, the seaweed appears, white against the bluest of blues. Every bubble and bobble, tendril and root, frizz and wrinkle is visible.

Father claps in delight.

1843—Anna's Book

Anna gazes at her seaweed cyanotype, fascinated by its detail. The blue background reminds her of the sea, the plant's natural habitat. She finds the image more truthful, more scientific, than any illustration she has ever seen.

She has a brilliant idea: a book! A book combining the science of botany with the realism of photography.

A book of her seaweed collection. No longer will it lie hidden in dark drawers. No one before has ever published a book of photographs. She will be the first!

Anna waits for the brightest of days. Some days Father helps. Some days her servants help. But the best days are when the weather helps. Only the sunniest days will activate the chemicals. And rain is all too frequent in England!

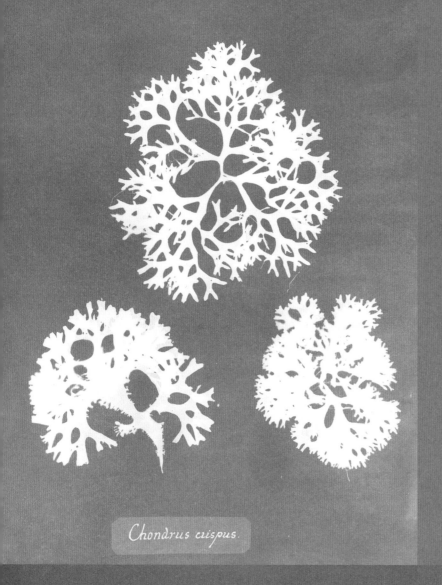

Chondrus crispus.

As Anna has so much seaweed, she decides to produce several volumes to document her entire collection.

She will label each type of seaweed with its Latin name so her work will be seen as a serious and useful endeavor by fellow botanists. In all she will make about two thousand prints over ten years. The first book is completed in 1843, when Anna is forty-four years old.

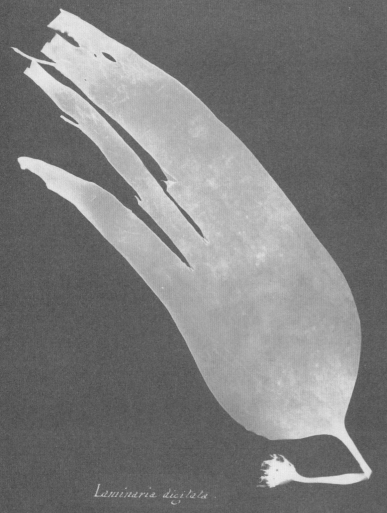

Laminaria digitata.

Fucus vesiculosus.

Alaria esculenta.

Halyseris polypodioides.

Rhodomenia laciniata.

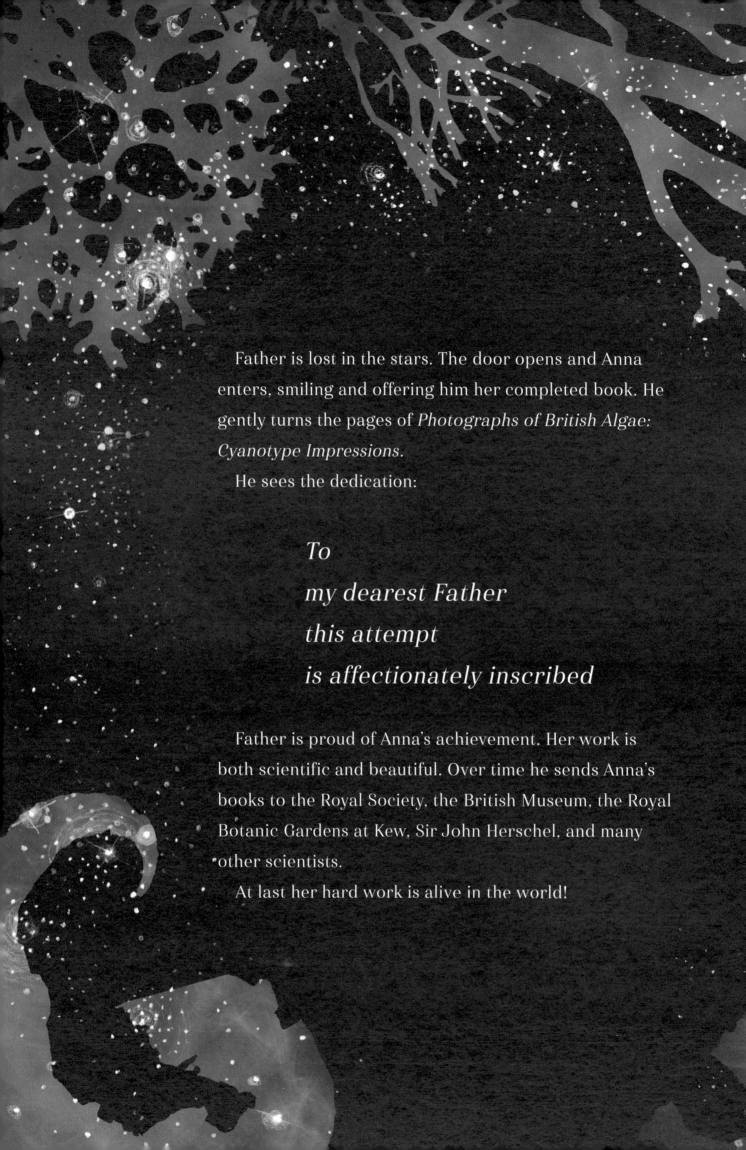

Father is lost in the stars. The door opens and Anna
enters, smiling and offering him her completed book. He
gently turns the pages of *Photographs of British Algae:
Cyanotype Impressions.*

He sees the dedication:

> *To*
>
> *my dearest Father*
>
> *this attempt*
>
> *is affectionately inscribed*

Father is proud of Anna's achievement. Her work is
both scientific and beautiful. Over time he sends Anna's
books to the Royal Society, the British Museum, the Royal
Botanic Gardens at Kew, Sir John Herschel, and many
other scientists.

At last her hard work is alive in the world!

1852—The Poppy

The sky is the bluest of blues. The air is thick with butterflies and bees. Anna drifts slowly, alone, through the tall grass.

Father has died.

A flash of bright red catches her eye. A poppy! She closes her eyes. A distant childhood memory sharpens into focus.

The poppy from that day with Father in the meadow, long ago. She wants the poppy to last forever.

In the dark, she coats a piece of paper with chemicals. She takes the paper outside and lays it down to bathe in the sun's rays. She places the poppy on the paper and places a sheet of glass on top. She waits a few minutes.

She removes the poppy and soaks the paper in water. As if by magic, the poppy appears, white against the bluest of blues.

Anna's "Poppy" cyanotype still exists and can be found in one of the
greatest museums in the world—the Victoria and Albert Museum in London.

Author's Note

Anna went on to make more books, including *Cyanotypes of British and Foreign Ferns* (1853) and *Cyanotypes of British and Foreign Flowering Plants and Ferns* (1854). She was helped by her friend Anne Dixon—a cousin of the novelist Jane Austen—who, along with Anna's husband, was greatly comforting to Anna after Father's death.

In 1853, Anna wrote and published a memoir of her father. She said of him, "Whatever he said or did was from the heart—there was no lukewarmness in him—whether friendship, science, or the wish to amuse a child was his object, the thing was undertaken and done *con amore.*" ("*Con amore*" means "with love" in Italian.)

She signed both this and *Photographs of British Algae: Cyanotype Impressions* with only her monogram, A.A. I sense she was quite shy; proud of her work, but having great humility. For years after her death, some people assumed that "A.A." meant "Anonymous Author." I suspect that the misunderstanding may have led to her being rarely acknowledged until historians of photography in the twentieth century further researched her beautiful and scientific books.

There is very little information about Anna as a child, so, for the first part of her biography, I focused on how she and Father may have spent time together. It is known that he greatly encouraged her education, especially in the sciences, and that her early years were spent in the beautiful Kent countryside. Collecting and preserving plants has always been a popular pastime in Great Britain, and especially in the nineteenth century. Flowers were often pressed and preserved between the pages of books. There were also many female seaweed hunters in this era, Queen Victoria being the most famous. At this time, trips to the seaside were thought to be restorative and invigorating, and nowhere in the British Isles is too far from the seashore!

No one knows the subject matter of Anna's very first cyanotype. I chose a seaweed to represent her experiment as her collection was massive.

Anna died at the age of seventy-two in 1871 and is buried near her home in Kent.

How to Make Your Own Cyanotypes

Cyanotypes are more commonly known as sun prints. Packs of chemically pre-treated paper with easy instructions are available at both art and photography supply stores and online.

To make your own chemically treated paper, you will need the help of an adult, as the chemicals are toxic and need to be handled carefully!

The chemical solution is an equal mixture of ferric ammonium citrate and potassium ferrocyanide, both of which should be diluted with water before mixing. The two diluted chemicals can be purchased online from Bostick & Sullivan, suppliers for alternative process photography, at bostick-sullivan.com.

While wearing gloves, mix the chemicals in a glass container. Apply the mixture with a wood and hair paintbrush to heavy watercolor paper in a dark, well ventilated room. (The brush should not have any metal parts, as the metal will interact with the chemicals!) Leave paper to dry in the dark for thirty minutes, then place in an envelope or box until ready to be used.

Flowers, leaves, feathers, buttons, keys, candies–any of your favorite treasures can be used to make the print. It's a good idea to practice arranging the composition before you make your print, as once the treated paper is in sunlight, you will only have a few seconds before the chemicals magically react. Like Anna, you should wait for the sunniest of days, have water at hand, and have fun experimenting!

Bibliography

Atkins, Anna (signed A.A.). *Photographs of British Algae: Cyanotype Impressions.* Self-published, 1843-1853.

———. *Memoir of J. G. Children, Esq.* Ulan Press, 2012.

Campbell-Culver, Maggie. *The Origin of Plants: The People and Plants That Have Shaped Britain's Garden History Since the Year 1000.* London: Headline, 2001.

Schaaf, Larry J. *Sun Gardens: Victorian Photographs by Anna Atkins.* New York: Aperture, 1985.

Institutions Holding Anna's Cyanotypes

Detroit Institute of Arts, Detroit, USA
Horniman Public Museum and Public Park Trust, London, UK
J. Paul Getty Museum, Los Angeles, USA
Kelvingrove Art Gallery and Museum, Glasgow, UK
Linnaen Society, London, UK
Metropolitan Museum of Art, New York, USA
Rijksmuseum, Amsterdam, Netherlands
Royal Botanic Garden, Edinburgh, UK
Royal Botanic Gardens, Kew, London, UK
Royal Society, London, UK
Spencer Collection, New York Public Library, New York, USA
Victoria and Albert Museum, London, UK

Please check before you visit that Anna's cyanotypes are on public display!

The New York Public Library's collection of Anna's work can be seen online at **digitalcollections.nypl.org**.

Acknowledgments

Thank you to Jay Zukerkorn especially for his expertise and kindness, for teaching me the rudiments of Photoshop, and for making this project a great experience. I am so grateful, too, for the support and ideas of the Abrams team: Susan Van Metre, Erica Finkel, Julia Marvel, Pamela Notarantonio, Erin Vandeveer, and Alison Gervais.

I'd also like to thank my agent, Paul Rodeen, for his support.

Thank you also to the Royal Botanic Gardens at Kew, London, and the Metropolitan Museum of Art, New York, both of which helped enormously with my research.

Illustration Credits

Cover: Anna's flower cyanotypes are from the J. Paul Getty Museum, Los Angeles, and her seaweed cyanotypes are from NYPL. **Pages 2-4:** "Drawings for Lamarck's Genera of Shells," 1823, courtesy of the Patrick Montgomery Collection. **Pages 35, 38, 39:** Photoshop-manipulated images are from the New York Public Library. **Pages 36, 37, 46, 47:** Anna's seaweed cyanotypes are from the New York Public Library, New York. **Page 42:** "Papaver Orientale," 1852-1854, © Victoria and Albert Museum, London.

To

my dearest Father

this attempt

is affectionately inscribed

–F.R.

Medium Note

The illustrations are montages of pencil drawings, watercolor paintings, vintage fabrics and wallpapers, wood veneers, and photographs. For example, in the English meadow, I first drew Anna, Father, and the butterflies. Then I painted the sky background. And then I took a walk in a *real* English meadow and collected grasses, buttercups, dandelions, clover, *everything*, and photographed them. I also used commonplace objects to represent some things. For example, in "Beside the Sea," I used a photograph of cling wrap to represent swirling, sparkling waves. On the cover, you can find a dragonfly and butterfly I created as cyanotypes in my own experimentation of the process. On page 34, I used one of my own cyanotypes of a pressed seaweed from the nineteenth century. I combined the drawn, painted, and photographed images together in Adobe Photoshop. These illustrations were so much fun to create! And I should say, of course, that Anna's art is represented in this book–please see Illustration Credits.

Cataloging-in-Publication Data has been applied for and may be obtained from the Library of Congress.

ISBN 978-1-4197-2551-7

Text and illustrations copyright © 2019 Fiona Robinson
Book design by Julia Marvel

Printed and bound in China
10 9 8 7 6 5 4

Abrams Books for Young Readers are available at special discounts when purchased in quantity for premiums and promotions as well as fundraising or educational use. Special editions can also be created to specification. For details, contact specialsales@abramsbooks.com or the address below.

Abrams® is a trademark of Harry N. Abrams, Inc.

ABRAMS The Art of Books
195 Broadway, New York, NY 10007
abramsbooks.com

Rhodomenia bifida.

Delesseria hypoglossum.

Schizonema cosmoides.

Enteromorpha compressa.

Fucus nodosus.

Enteromorpha intestinalis.

Dictyosiphon foeniculaceus.

Laminaria bulbosa.

Furcellaria fastigiata.

Ceramium rubrum var.

Rhodomenia reniformis.

Delesseria sanguinea aculeata.

Codium bursa.

Padina Pavonia.

Zygnema nitidum.

Desmidia filiformis.